Copyright © 2022 Michèle Saint-Michel
All rights reserved.
10 9 8 7 6 5 4 3 2 1

Published by Bad Saturn. BAD SATURN and associated logos are trademarks and/ or registered trademarks.

All rights reserved under International and Pan-American Copyright Conventions. No part of this publication may be reproduced, transmitted, downloaded, decompiled, reverse engineered, or stored in or introduced into any information storage and retrieval system, in any form or by any means, whether electronic or mechanical, now known or hereafter invented, without the express written permission of the publisher. For information regarding permissions, email Bad Saturn, Attention: Permissions Department.

The publisher does not have any control over and does not assume any responsibility for author or third-party websites or their content.

LIBRARY OF CONGRESS
CATALOGING-IN-PUBLICATION DATA

Saint-Michel, Michèle.
A Journal of Gigantic Beauty: A Lined Journal
/ by Michèle Saint-Michel.
— 1st ed.
p.
Crn.
ISBN: 978-0-9999020-5-9

Summary:
A lined journal with room to daydream. Based on the work of artist and poet Michèle Saint-Michel, this lined journal creates space for thoughts, observations, and poetry. For anyone who sees extraordinary beauty in the everyday.

I skirt sierras
my palms cover continents,
Absorbing all to myself

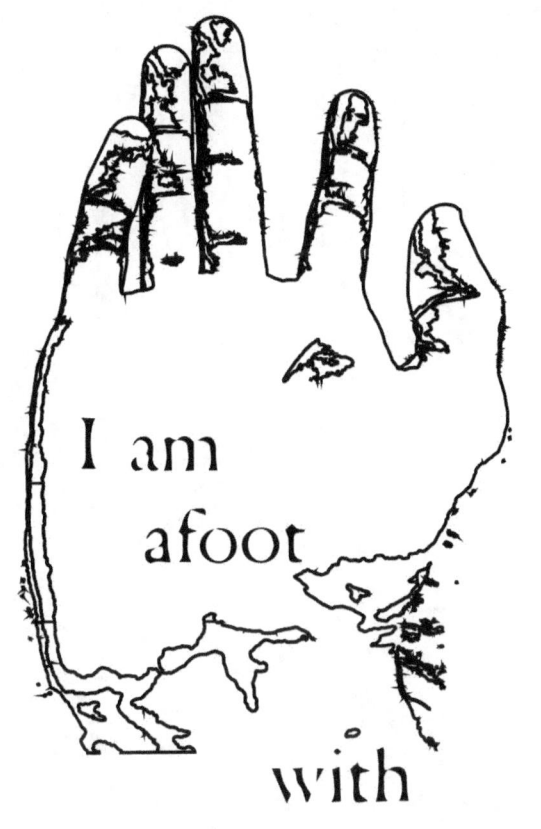

I am
afoot

with

my vision.

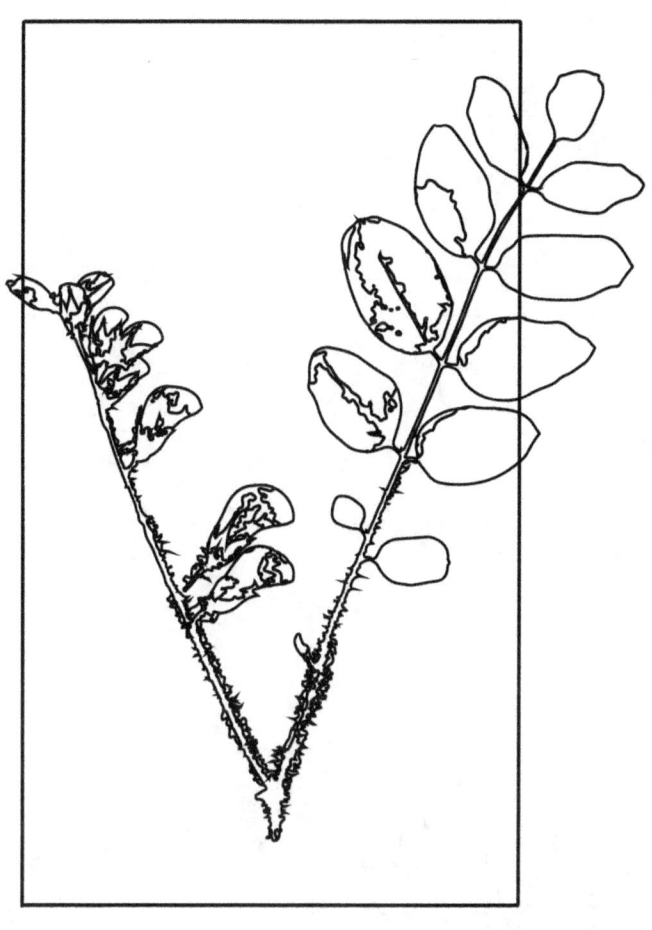

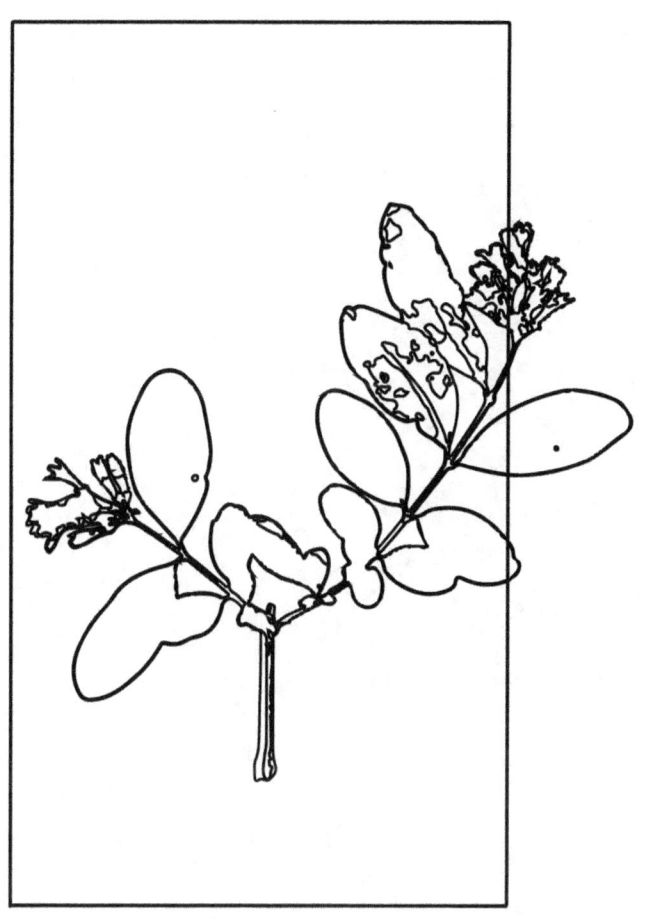

My ties and ballasts leave me,
 my elbows rest in sea-gaps,
I skirt sierras
 my palms cover continents,
 I am
  afoot
   with
    my vision.

a lined journal with room to daydream

For anyone who sees extraordinary beauty in the everyday, this lined journal creates space for thoughts, observations, and poetry.

...

This collection of journals is punctuated by the words of Walt Whitman. The poet's work was a pillar of Saint-Michel's erasure and concrete poetry collection, *Saint Agatha Mother Redeemer*. Working closely with the text created an intimacy in particular with his magnum opus, *Leaves of Grass*. Though it was first published in 1855, Whitman spent most of his professional life writing and rewriting the epic work. Take a page from Whitman and continue writing and rewriting your own story.

Buy or gift Michèle Saint-Michel's books to experience words and worlds with new eyes.

...

Also by Michèle Saint-Michel

Experiments in Dreaming: A Lined Journal

Journeywork of the Stars: A Dotted Journal

Grief Is an Origami Swan

*Saint Agatha Mother Redeemer:
A Survivor's Story in the Words of Dead Poets*

Saint Agatha Mother Redeemer Coloring Book

Liner Notes for Getting Out Without Catching Fire

v

www.ingramcontent.com/pod-product-compliance
Lightning Source LLC
Chambersburg PA
CBHW070432010526
44118CB00014B/2012